PICTURE LIBRARY

POISONOUS SNAKES

POISONOUS SNAKES

Norman Barrett

Franklin Watts

New York London Toronto Sydney

©1991 Franklin Watts

Franklin Watts, Inc.
387 Park Avenue South
New York, NY 10016

Printed in the United Kingdom

Library of Congress Cataloging-in-Publication Data

Barrett, Norman S.
    Poisonous snakes/Norman Barrett.
        p. cm. — (Picture library)
    Includes index.
    Summary: Describes a variety of venomous snakes from around the
    world and discusses their habitats, how they produce poison, and
    their natural enemies.
    ISBN 0-531-14153-5
    1. Poisonous snakes — Juvenile literature. [1. Poisonous snakes.
    2. Snakes.]
    I. Title. II. Series.
    QL666.O6B327 1991
    597.96—dc20
                                                90-46109
                                                CIP AC

Designed by
Barrett and Weintroub

Research by
Deborah Spring

Picture Research by
Ruth Sonntag

Photographs by
Heather Angel/Brian Rogers (front)
    cover, page 23)
Australian Overseas Information
    Service, London (page 15t)
S.C. Bisserot (pages 2, 3, 7, 11, 12, 24t
    26, 27, 30t)
Michael Chinery (page 28)
Pat Morris (pages 10, 19t, 20b, 21t, 30b
    back cover)
Natural Science Photos (page 25)
Queensland Tourist and Travel
    Corporation (page 15b)
Survival Anglia (pages 6, 13, 14, 16, 17
    18, 19b, 20t, 21b, 22, 24b, 29, 30m)

Illustration by
Rhoda and Robert Burns

Technical Consultant
Michael Chinery

Contents

Introduction

Snakes are reptiles, like lizards and crocodiles. They feed on other animals. They eat mammals such as mice, rabbits and even small antelope. Some snakes eat fish, lizards, frogs, or other snakes.

Some snakes use venom, or poison, to kill their prey before eating it. They bite their prey with fangs and inject the venom. This either kills or paralyzes the prey, and the snake then swallows it whole.

△ A black spitting cobra from eastern Africa. Cobras inject their prey with venom. Spitting cobras are so called because, when attacked, they spit venom into the eyes of their enemies. This causes great pain and temporary blindness.

There are three main kinds of poisonous snakes. The elapid family includes cobras and mambas. Adders and rattlesnakes belong to the viper family. Elapids and vipers are front-fanged snakes. The third group are the back-fanged snakes.

Poisonous snakes live mainly in warm or tropical lands, but most countries have some snakes. Only a few kinds of poisonous snakes are dangerous to people.

△ A pit viper coiled around a branch. Vipers are known for the speed with which they strike at their prey, much quicker than the other kinds of poisonous snakes.

Looking at poisonous snakes

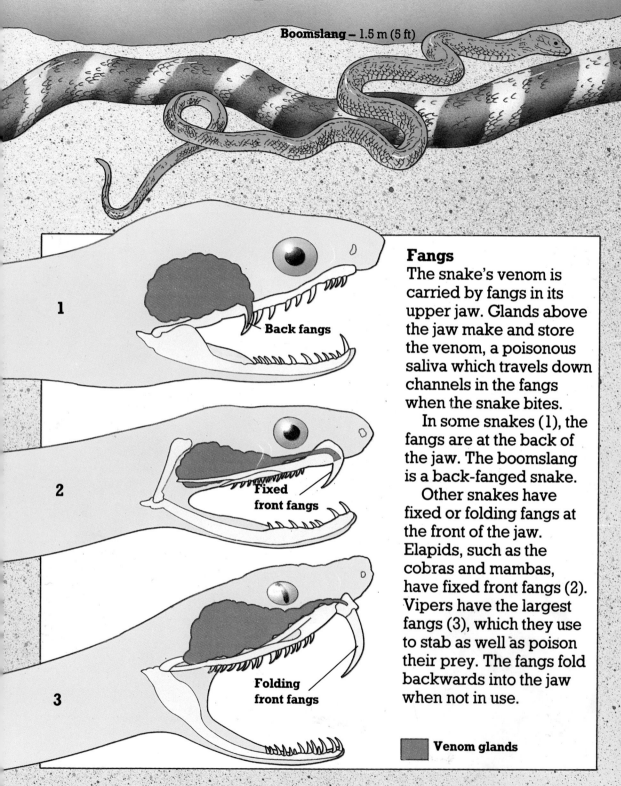

Boomslang – 1.5 m (5 ft)

1 Back fangs

2 Fixed front fangs

3 Folding front fangs

Fangs

The snake's venom is carried by fangs in its upper jaw. Glands above the jaw make and store the venom, a poisonous saliva which travels down channels in the fangs when the snake bites.

In some snakes (1), the fangs are at the back of the jaw. The boomslang is a back-fanged snake.

Other snakes have fixed or folding fangs at the front of the jaw. Elapids, such as the cobras and mambas, have fixed front fangs (2). Vipers have the largest fangs (3), which they use to stab as well as poison their prey. The fangs fold backwards into the jaw when not in use.

◼ Venom glands

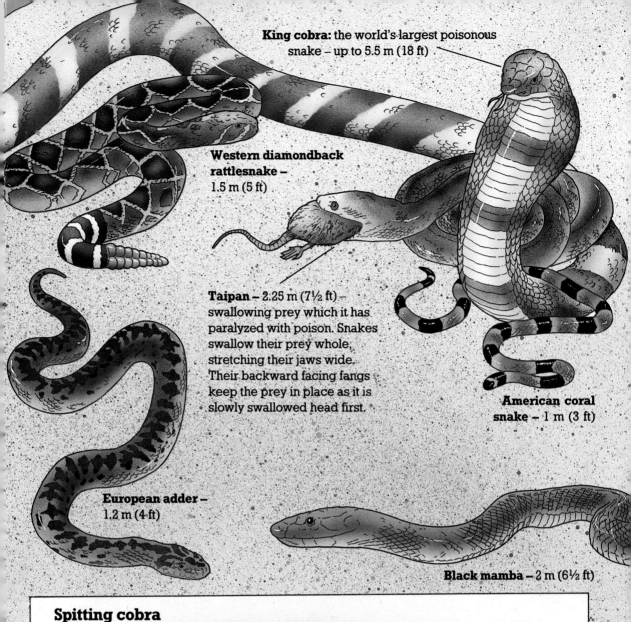

King cobra: the world's largest poisonous snake – up to 5.5 m (18 ft)

Western diamondback rattlesnake – 1.5 m (5 ft)

Taipan – 2.25 m (7½ ft) – swallowing prey which it has paralyzed with poison. Snakes swallow their prey whole, stretching their jaws wide. Their backward facing fangs keep the prey in place as it is slowly swallowed head first.

American coral snake – 1 m (3 ft)

European adder – 1.2 m (4 ft)

Black mamba – 2 m (6½ ft)

Spitting cobra

The spitting cobra rears up and shoots a jet of venom at its enemy's eyes. It can spit venom as far as 2.5 m (8 ft).

Cobras and other elapids

Cobras are found in open country throughout most of Asia, where they live in holes in the ground. They are normally found on the ground, but in the tropical forests of Africa, live in the trees.

Cobras eat small mammals such as rodents, and might eat small birds from a nest in a shrub. The huge king cobra eats only other species of snakes.

Most species of elapids hatch from eggs.

△ The Mozambique cobra is one of the spitting cobras. These animals can spray venom to a distance of about 2.5 m (8 ft).

▷ The monocled cobra of Asia in defensive pose. When threatened, cobras spread their hoods to look fierce. They usually try to escape from danger, but when they do strike they can be deadly.

△ The green mamba lives mainly in trees, where it glides rapidly along the branches. Like the other three species of mambas, its bite is deadly, but it is not an aggressive snake.

◁ The banded krait also has a highly poisonous bite, but is a timid creature and will hide its head under its body when frightened. Kraits feed only on other snakes.

The mambas are the fastest of the poisonous snakes. The black mamba has a reputation for being aggressive, and is one of the most feared snakes in Africa. Yet mambas are usually timid, and will flee rather than attack an intruder.

Another deadly elapid is the krait. There are several species, all from Asia. They are very timid unless provoked. They are most dangerous at night, when their bold colors are less easily seen.

▽ The yellow-bellied sea snake. There are nearly 50 species of sea snake, found mainly in tropical waters along Pacific and Indian Ocean coastlines. These close relatives of the elapids are well adapted to life in the seas. They have a flattened tail, like an oar, which they use to drive themselves through the water. They live on fish, and bear live young.

No elapids are found in Europe. The brightly banded coral snakes are the only elapids that live in the Americas. They are burrowing snakes with short fangs, and most species are small.

Australia has more than eighty species of elapids, many of them fairly harmless. The rare taipan, however, has a deadly bite. Other dangerous Australian elapids include the death adder, tiger snake, copperhead and brown snake.

△ A coral snake of North and Central America, with its typical pattern of red, black and yellow bands. Coral snakes live on small snakes and lizards. They are usually placid, but have a deadly bite, which they use if disturbed. Some non-poisonous snakes have a similar color pattern, but with the red and black bands next to each other. North American coral snakes have the red and yellow bands together.

▷ The tiger snake is one of the deadliest snakes in the world. It is not aggressive, but is a large snake and is feared in parts of Australia, especially the southeast, where it is abundant. Tiger snakes give birth to live young.

▽ The bandy bandy is found in most parts of Australia. It is a burrowing snake not more than 40 cm (16 in) long.

Rattlesnakes and other vipers

The viper family has about 150 species and is fairly widespread around the world. It is divided into two groups.

The pit vipers, found mainly in the Americas and southeastern Asia, include the rattlesnakes. The true vipers range from the common European adder to the deadly African puff adder.

Most viper species live on the ground and give birth to live young.

▷ A rattlesnake poised to strike. Vipers strike with deadly speed. Most vipers have a short, thick body, a narrow neck and an arrow-shaped head. A rattlesnake's rattle is at the end of its tail. It creates a buzzing noise, thought to be a warning to enemies.

▽ Prairie rattlesnakes around their den in the southwestern desert of the United States.

True vipers live in Europe, Africa, Asia and the East Indies. The European viper, or adder, is found farther north than any other species of snake. Adders may even be found beyond the Arctic Circle, in Scandinavia. They hibernate during the winter in the cooler regions.

The most southerly snake is the snout-headed lancehead, a South American pit viper found well down into Argentina.

△ A diamondback rattlesnake eating a rabbit. Diamondbacks are considered the most dangerous of the poisonous snakes in the United States.

▷ The puff adder is one of the most dangerous snakes in Africa. It lives in open country, where it is well camouflaged, and feeds on small mammals.

▽ The gaboon viper lives in the forests and is the largest viper in Africa, over 1.5 m (5 ft) long. It has the longest fangs of any snake, more than 2.5 cm (1 in) long. It is highly poisonous, but fairly placid.

▷ An adder flicks its tongue out. Snakes do this to pick up the scent of their prey. The adder is the only poisonous snake found in the British Isles.

▽ The asp, similar in size to the adder, may be recognized by its slightly upturned snout. It is also a true viper, and is found in central and western Europe. It is not to be confused with the Egyptian cobra, which is also sometimes known as an asp.

△ A pit viper from Malaysia. This close-up clearly shows the "pits," just in front of the eyes. These are organs that enable the snake to detect prey by its body heat.

▽ The cottonmouth, or water moccasin, is a dangerous pit viper found in the swamps and streams of the southern United States. It feeds mainly on fish and amphibians.

Back-fanged snakes

Back-fanged snakes inject venom slowly as they chew their prey. Few back-fanged snakes are harmful to people. Two exceptions are the boomslang and the vine, or twig, snake of Africa. Neither are aggressive snakes, but their bite is highly poisonous.

The venom of some back-fanged snakes is particularly poisonous for the prey on which they feed, whether it be other snakes, frogs or even crabs.

▷ A parrot snake from the forests of Costa Rica in an aggressive mood. Most kinds of back-fanged snakes are tree-dwellers.

▽ A brown water snake swallowing a catfish in the Florida Everglades. These snakes are not strictly classed as poisonous. But their saliva enters the prey through puncture wounds caused by their teeth, and this has a paralyzing effect.

△ The boomslang is one of the few back-fanged snakes whose bite can be dangerous to people.

◁ A boomslang eats a bird after raiding its nest. The boomslang is typical of back-fanged snakes – long, slim and well camouflaged among the branches of trees.

Enemies of snakes

Animals that prey on poisonous snakes have to be quick or well protected to avoid getting bitten.

The mongoose is well known for battling its traditional enemy, the cobra. Other mammals, too, such as the meerkat and some wild cats prey on snakes. The king cobra and the coral snake eat other snakes.

Many eagles include snakes in their diet, and some prey only on snakes. The secretary bird is among the deadliest of snake-killers.

▽ A secretary bird attacks and kills a puff adder. Unlike eagles, these African birds of prey do not swoop down on their victims from the air. They prefer to run along the ground and trample on their prey, protected by hard scales on their long legs.

Snakes and people

People are the snake's biggest enemy. Largely because of a fear of snakes, people in many parts of the world treat them as objects of hate, whether they are poisonous or not.

Many snakes are killed for their skins or for meat. But the greatest danger to snakes, as to many other animals, is the destruction of their habitats as people intrude on rainforests and other wild places.

△ Schoolchildren watch a demonstration of snake-handling at a snake park. However expert they are, snake handlers treat poisonous snakes with great respect.

People keep poisonous snakes in captivity for a number of reasons.

Scientists use snake venom to produce drugs needed to treat various illnesses. They also make "antivenin" for the treatment of snakebite.

Zoos and reptile houses keep poisonous snakes, which are among the most popular exhibits.

In parts of Asia and North Africa, snakes feature in snake-charming and other forms of entertainment.

▽ Snake charmers in Sri Lanka, one with a non-venomous python wrapped around his neck. As seen here, cobras are the most popular snakes for these shows. They are supposed to "dance" to the sound of the music. But snakes are deaf to airborne sounds. They move around as they follow the movement of the charmer and his flute. Some snake charmers are known to pull out the fangs of their snakes and mistreat them in other ways.

The story of poisonous snakes

The perfect predators

Snakes became plentiful on earth about 60 or 70 million years ago. They probably evolved (developed over millions of years) from burrowing lizards. They became very efficient hunters, or predators, using stealth and camouflage to creep up on their prey or to hide from animals that preyed on them.

Some snakes developed poison fangs. This weapon enabled them to become the perfect predators. They can strike swiftly and with deadly accuracy, often without even being seen. Then they can wait in safety as their prey weakens before swallowing it and returning to a safe place to digest it.

Snakes in ancient times

Snakes, especially poisonous ones, have always been objects of fear and wonder. They figured strongly in ancient beliefs. According to the Bible, it was the serpent in the Garden of Eden that tempted Eve, and God then punished it by taking away its legs.

The snake's ability to shed its skin whole and come out looking like a new snake led ancient peoples to think snakes never died. Their ability to strike and kill a human being made them seem superhuman, and many early peoples worshipped them. The ancient Egyptians believed that their gods were descended from snakes.

△ "Milking" venom from a cobra. Snake venom is used in making drugs.

Uses of poisonous snakes

People used to believe that snakes had magical properties. Early doctors in Europe prepared potions from snakes' bodies that were supposed to cure all kinds of illnesses and defects. The snake was held in such high regard in medicine that it became the symbol of the medical profession. Even today snake venom has important uses in the preparation of some modern drugs.

In some places, such as Japan, sea snakes are eaten as a delicacy. Snakeskin is used in the manufacture of shoes and other clothing, and some snakes have been hunted almost to extinction for this purpose.

Protection

Snakes need protection from unnecessary killing and ill-treatment just as other animals do. The extermination of poisonous snakes can lead to other problems. After the elimination of poisonous snakes in parts of Thailand recently, many farming areas have been overrun with rodents and other pests.

Cruelty to snakes is no more excusable than it would be to other forms of wildlife. In some parts of the United States the people hold rattlesnake round-ups. About 30 of these noisy festivals take place every year, mostly in the southern states. The idea is for hunters to catch as many rattlesnakes as they can. They often do this by pouring or pumping gasoline into holes where the snakes live. All the

snakes caught are kept in pits or large containers. Large numbers of people watch as wriggling snakes are taken from the containers to have their heads chopped off or to be abused in other ways. The people enjoy all kinds of other entertainment at the expense of the poor creatures, as well as eating cooked rattlesnake meat.

△ A snake handler tips another batch of rattlesnakes into the "pit." Some people get pleasure from watching snakes being ill-treated and killed in jamborees called rattlesnake round-ups.

Facts and records

△ A prairie rattlesnake's rattle. A new ring is added every time the snake sheds its skin.

Rattle

A rattlesnake's rattle is made up of a series of horny rings loosely locked together. Every time the snake sheds its skin, a new ring is added – two to four times a year. But few rattles consist of more than about 10–12 rings, because they begin to fall off at that stage.

△ The black mamba – said to be the world's fastest snake.

Fastest

Stories of the speed of snakes are often exaggerated. The black mamba is thought to be the fastest-moving snake, reaching speeds of 20 km/h (12 mph) for short distances.

△ The king cobra – the world's largest poisonous snake.

Largest

The largest poisonous snake is the king cobra. Some of these creatures measure as much as 5.5 m (18 ft) long.

Glossary

Antivenin
A drug that stops the effects of a venom.

Back-fanged snakes
A group of snakes with fangs at the back of their mouth. They continue to bite their prey to inject more venom.

Camouflage
Coloring, shape and skin markings that help an animal to blend in with its surroundings and hide from its prey and its enemies.

Elapids
The family of poisonous snakes that includes cobras, mambas, taipans, tiger snakes and sea snakes.

Extermination
The killing off of certain animals in a particular area.

Extinction
The dying out of a species.

Fangs
Teeth through which poisonous snakes inject their prey with venom.

Habitat
The surroundings in which a particular species lives. Habitat includes climate, character of the land or water, and other animal or plant life present.

Pit vipers
Members of the viper family with "pits" near their eyes. The snakes detect their prey or possible enemies through these pits by sensing their body heat. Rattlesnakes are pit vipers.

Predators
Animals that catch and eat other creatures.

True vipers
Members of the viper family that are not pit vipers. They include adders and asps.

Venom
A poison that can be ejected into or squirted at prey or enemies.

Vipers
The family of poisonous snakes that includes adders and rattlesnakes. Vipers have long, hinged fangs at the front of the mouth.

Index